MW01688724

INNER LIGHT
PUBLICATIONS

Surfacing

A Poetic Journey of The Self

By

Karuna Devi

Surfacing: A Poetic Journey of The Self

Cover art by Ilia Pasymansky
Text layout and Graphic Design by Elizabeth Nichols

ISBN-10: 0-9790566-0-8
ISBN-13: 978-0-9790566-0-4

Library of Congress Control Number: 2006936795

Printed in Canada.

Innerlight Publications
Forest Hills, NY
www.innerlight-publications.com

~ dedication ~

to my guruji
who taught me to believe
in my Self

Acknowledgments

There is an African proverb which says: It takes a village to raise a child. This also is true for raising any project or plan from when it is conceived as Idea to its material state. I would like to acknowledge some of the members of my village beginning with Hrishikesh who for the past eleven years has encouraged me to keep writing; to keep reaching towards the inner light and to share the secrets of The Heart with others. Without his generosity and support, *Surfacing* would not have been possible. A deep gratitude goes to Elizabeth whose skill and reliability along with her genuine enthusiasm were so fundamental to seeing this project through. Also, I wish to extend sincere thanks to Ilia for adding such beauty to this work by his colorful cover art. For patiently creating so many OMs, suns and symbols for us.

Namastee!

108 Poems

Praseed	1
Bare Bones	3
In Captivity	4
Mouna	5
Where We Ride	6
Reeling in the Ocean	8
Closer Than You Think	10
Existence	11
Golden Errand	12
The Thought Keepers	13
Tracks For Your Train	14
Love's Arms	15
Who Am I	16
Enraptured in the Stream of Heavenly Fellowship	18
Imagine	19
Time	20
Brahman of the Upanishads	22
This Thirst	23
Guru	24
Fear	26
Breath	28
If I Meet You	29
The Sapera's Song	30
Yes	31
River Song	32
The Dream	33
A Fist Full of Chickpeas	34
Flower of Compassion	35
The Disciple	36
In the Range of Fire	38

Hourglass 39
Banyan 40
The Sleeper 41
The Shadow 42
Substance 44
Two Ways 45
Prudence 46
Mother, It Is Thy Mercy 47
Looking Beyond 49
How Can It Be 50
In Many a Crusading Hour 51
Unhidden 52
The Myth of Man 53
Man, Oh Man 54
Goodbye 55
Him 57
My Dreams 58
Divded Nation 59
The Third Day 60
Unity 61
Spirit 62
Offering 63
Butterfly Spirit 64
Great is the Man 65
The Inner Mystic 66
Vedanta 68
Tending the Fire 69
Surface Trade 71
One Turn 73
Wishing Well 75
Release 76
Word Sculpture 77
The Impeller 78
No Words 79

The Smallest Fraction 80
Under the Almond Tree 81
What Fears 83
Inconsequential Things 84
The Desert Must Be Known 86
Life 88
The One Waits 90
Crossroads 92
Evolution 94
By Grace 95
The Cosmic Echo 98
Heart's Desire 100
Rusted Nail 102
Something Less Vulnerable 103
Chant 105
Forever Full 106
Asana 107
Revelation 109
The Dragon's Lair 111
Soul (Jiva) 113
Grit 115
If You Dare 116
Strike the Drum 117
Grain of Rice 119
Voices of Vedanta 120
Dissolution and Glory 122
Rosary of Souls 123
Lotus 124
Havan of the Heart 126
There Is Enough 128
Touching Down to Fly 130
Two Birds 131
Plato's Cave 132
The Way of the Bodhisattva 134

Mere Speculation	135
Song of Moses	137
Both Weak and Strong	140
Carry Me Away	142
Hills of Frankincense	144
Lost in the Majesty	146
Forever Untouched	148
Presence and Need	149
Tadvanam	151
Surfacing	153
The Dialogue	157
Glossary	161

I have been drifting from darkness to passion, from passion to darkness. Shaking off evil, as a horse shakes off his loose hair, freeing myself from evil as the moon breaks free from the exlipse, attaining the aim of my life, I enter the Kingdom of Heaven, where there is nothing more to attain; I enter the Kingdom of Heaven.

~ from the Chandogya Upanishad ~

Praseed

It is a clean and quiet page
so I lay down my mat,
because the grass that is crushed
will rise again.

To that gracious, non-dual
One Thus Gone,
I offer salutations again and again.
May these beads roll
into the amber arms of the Omkarum.

In the light of yoga
the indweller is lit
and burns in its own
essential oil.

There, the river of saints
has many hands but only one
fountainhead,
And it flows like Rishikesh
through the festival in our heart.

There, Earth's opal is borne
on the fiery hood of confluent waters.

Oh Devi, you are the eloquence of that river.
Oh Devi, be pleased and find for us
our work!
For your banner decorates every mansion door
and you goad all souls with your
lotus and dagger.

Where do we begin?

In the tears of Rudra,
we are the salt of longing and the
pupil in his eye.
Our words and breath together cave in
under the wealth of his endless repetition.

Truly, all creation slithers like a snake
and waits to be charmed
out of its skin.

But at the root of my burn
rains a benediction,
"Please be receptive to what proceeds."

My teacher's words have sown the seeds
and bleed with Shiva's sanguine lines.
Oh Heart, catch the thrust of His hunter's spear
and without hesitation, let this japa commence.

Bare Bones

Oh dear reader,
I have been to lands of light
and perched weightless
in the nook of a thought.

I have enjoyed the power
apart from the sting
as a winged designer
of an untouched plan.

I have sat in the nucleus of desire
and felt satiated a thousand times over
where sorrows seemed to disperse
in the winds pushed up by a dream.

But in a lucid hour not far gone,
I have come to know all good merits rest
in the timid flash
of a candle's flame.

So light the wick of your will
while there is wax to burn.
For there is only bare bones in Prometheus's gift,
unless you give up the good and catch a fire.

In Captivity

Love gathers.
Call it Govinda for He is
cowherder, heartherder,
corraler of souls.

To my one sole desire,
you are free to leave,
but you are like the one in the
unicorn tapestry who stays tethered
to the pomegranate tree.

Love bewitches and heals.
Even in this rebellious, uncertain hour
my last love song amidst its reveling is
overcome
and like a weak bird, returns.

Mouna

Words are but

fragmented

unfocused thoughts
that click clack from the
factory of

eddying ideas blowing up

dust

and the mind in his
mental prowess

forgets the

silence.

Where We Ride

For these initiated years we have been
riders on the black winds
of midnight-The Path Unseen.

Because there is no cool breeze coming
off the dusty hooves of the stampede.

Because even the ecliptic reins know
we are creatures of space.

Where we go is determined by where
we lean-but these words are symbols
for symbols in the pyramid of the heart
where it is written-
Enter, descend and only then rise up!

My brother, we must believe
our destiny is the poetry
of night-blooming jasmine.
For these years with Krishna have come
as a friend.
Remember His circle of spinning saris and know
we have chosen the surest course.

This dark tunnel is lined with doors
all opening to the light of His face.
Throughout its corridors, the nightingale sings!

Oh Hrishikesh, there is still time
for our bright future.
Let us synchronize our Selves to
His music, like the swinging strings
of a damaru-

Where our joined hearts form the
knot that sounds,

Where an inner voice whispers Truths
to humanity,

Where Shiva and Shakti dance in
union divine,

And where one plus one,
like a prophet's bread and fish,
bountifully equals eleven!

Reeling in the Ocean

I am caught on the very hook of that
question-when did you start reeling me in?

There are no fish here, only waters
being mixed with waters
and I feel my name disappear
in a tonic for the nameless drinker to drink.

Everything temporary serves as bait
to lead us towards the permanent.
Even distant stars can die before their light
reaches our eyes,
But not so for the light which shines
in a bakti's eyes-that light is effulgence
that light is breathless bliss.

Philosophers ponder with twisted faces
speaking of lofty transformation,
But one heated look from a holy man would
remind anyone of their thirst.
Then the milk of their soul would boil,
and they would hand over their heart
like a coconut to be cracked.

What is real puts an end to the possession
of moods and questions.
I have felt what is real
surface
from time to time, like a fin sharply parting
my waters.

It is my Kailash, who divines from a crystal
mountain
as a moon, an egg, an eye.
His secrets fish this universe
for the Truth let out in a cry.

That is why Love says it is good
to be gotten,
because every passion played before the reeler
makes a tight line from the saffron
folds of a gifted heart.

Closer Than You Think

Stubbornly loveless, restless,
moving from extreme to extreme,
You fear to face the current of change.
But there is a revolution in your heart
and it will call to the surface your unvoiced cry.
It will serve you to suffer the pain.

When you experience that emptiness
with the length and breadth of your heart,
the four-fold goal of human existence
is closer than you think.

Existence

O Great Brahma, you
illuminate the colors in my heart,
may they ever shine in light
forms pleasing to you.
Beyond ephemeral conditions
you stand alone.
Creator of laws, of time, of planets, of souls, of
nothing too.

O Holy Vishnu, I
float in the sea foam of your existence
for Maya is your
clever daughter.
Preserver of memory, virtues, vices, of hearts and of
nothing too.

O Hoary Shiva, your presence
is inevitable!
Mountains shake as you dance.
Nataraja, let the walls crack
and the birth of death begin.
Destroyer of earth, of stars, of space, of present and
of nothing too.

Golden Errand

These visions come
like a gentle dove
to perch upon my lowly spoken shoulders.

And though there is room to get lost
in the light which flashes
in one of its rays,
My soul tells my not to kneel nor yield,
but question the direction
from which it came.

For it has seen every message-bearing thought
sprout wings,
and push off from the strong arm
of my Prince.

And it knows it was He who sent thee
on thy swift flight
across resurrected space.
My mind holds that place
as a means to an end.

So before this pigeon, I place no palanquin
but keep my sight
on the distant wind.

You did glide your life on His
generous breath,
but I cannot find my rest on your
golden errand.

The Thought Keepers

We are the thought keepers,
preserving Nature's upward rain
as it floods space with light and color.

For his ascension we breathe into man
an endless end.
He does not see his mind made it so.

We know. All this talk of surfacing belongs to
The Self
We say-Selah-and sing a new psalm.
For The Self will edify all in the end.
He does not see the law made it so.

We string deeds, like beads, on the ether.
We wear a garland of stars on our neck.
Neither vow nor verse can weigh us down.
He does not see our God made it so.

Man is the ocean inside of the fish
who is blind yet underlying knows.
But there is no keeping mind on a silver dish

so we travel through the stream of the heart,
where a window is a mirror,
and what we see is too bright to behold
in the orb of an eye.

Tracks For Your Train

We are all daughters and rivers
and lovers of Thee.

All of our offerings are indeed
your whisperings where
Sita is the river, and Ram is the sea.

We are all children and mountains
and secrets of Thee.
And I know that we forever fail
in our approach, for whatever we lay out
it is only tracks for your train.

There is nothing else
and nothing to surface
except for the eye of a harvest moon.

Like saffron, it shines on the pale of the sea
where gypsies of change make one
phase of our heart. For free is your lila
longing to play as

Goddess and inlets
and pendulums of the Thee,
with the white beam of our soul caught
in the prism of your love.

Love's Arms

Oh Love, you lay coiled up
but my heart is on the hunt
and your feathers are fit
into my bow.

Love, you are the living arrow
for which my whole body bends
begging to spring
from Yama's taut draw.

The gazelle of my soul can wait
no more,
she longs to run
and you are her speed.

Race swiftly up this road
to God
and release a thousand Africas
from my breast.

What lives in love, my heart cannot say
for love is its voice and its light,
its target and its steady aim, its fired flame
and alas, its empty quiver.

Who Am I

I am fathers and forefathers from long ago,
the habits that chain me,
the character that frames me,
the silent thoughts I'd never show.

Who am I?
I am your cousin your sister,
your lover your mother,
your healer your deceiver,
your cover your revealer.

Who am I?
I am the floating salt of the ocean,
the smell of moss,
the sound of rain.
I am one thousand shades of green.
I am the red of Utah.

I crawl on and inside the earth.
Swim in her watery belly.
Fly to her mountain peaks and gaze in silence.

I grow up from the cracks of rocks.
From barren sands I quench my thirst.
From black mud I rise and float white.

Who am I?
I live in the mouth of the liar,
the loins of the lustful,
the hands that are stained with another man's
blood.

Yes I am there...
on the street,
in an alley,
sitting at the corner bar.

Who am I?
I am the forgiver.
I am the redeemer.
I am the sustainer.

Who am I?
I am the one in the many,
the many in the one.
The laughter in silence,
the motion in stillness.
The valor in the fainthearted,
the hidden love in harshness.
The equilibrium amidst the chaos.

I am life-affirming passage of death.
I am the junction between possibility and

Triumph.

Enraptured in the Stream of Heavenly Fellowship

Experience only
satisfies the soul.

Weary am I
of speculation.

That is why I have remained.

In your company
I have learned
a gainful passion,

the kind that transmutes men
into gold.

You are The Stone
Self is my stream,
all this is alchemy
of the Heart.

But since neither experience
nor heavenly fellowship
deal in words,

my God-what can I say

As Kailashananda
fills the pit
of people, places and things

leaving this eternal mysticism
without a hole
to lie and hide.

Imagine

Lord, I call to you.
In blindness we strive to see where you are.
Will your grace save us from this vision of division?
I know not how it feels to have peace
Nor joy
Nor fearlessness

And sometimes I dare to imagine what that is like,
as the caterpillar imagines the butterfly.

Time

The myriad of conditions
they come and pass away;
Of works that yield fruition
never long do stay.

Moments freely given
days are yours to seize;
Histories are written
years blow in the breeze.

Are you not the taker?
This worldly life you claim,
then toss us to our maker
divest of body and name.

You take the beauty from the flower,
the flower of our youth.
You turn the mountains into powder,
and grind the seed to root.

Claiming monarchs, emperors
Kingdoms in their glory;
Dethrone them all, leave no heirs
reduce them to a story.

You take the mother from the child,
child from the mother.
Ignoring hearts with skillful style
parting love from lover.

Surely as the solid earth
through desert oceans change,
pulsing blood of life from birth
will dry up in our veins.

Legends lived before us
from where now do they dwell?
Bones decay to dust
and Time will never tell.

Hover every hour,
stalking all of life.
Slowly you devour,
aeons fall to blight.

Who but few dare travel
beyond your measured line,
where illusion does unravel
in the grandeur of design.

In that place Eternity
dethrones Time of her glory;
Turns destruction back to space
and sanctifies her fury.

Brahman of the Upanishads

Brahman of the Upanishads,
lead me to your secret place-
Where the saints rejoice in your glory
Where the Heavenly Fathers take delight
Where even the haughty lower their heads.

Brahman of the Upanishads,
lead me to your secret place-
Where all hearts beat in unison OM.
Where the living reside in joy
Where peace is the unspoken language.

Brahman of the Upanishads,
lead me to your secret place-
Where all are free from suffering
Where worldly shackles fall off
Where darkness exists no more.

In that sacred place, may the essence of my life melt
in the fountain flowing from your feet.

This Thirst

The first shall be the last.
All this pain-like water
splashing about.

Many rise up, only to fall.

All part according to their karmas,
All leave the jiva
without a home.

What plan has He
who harnessed the ocean
with bridle and bit,
with bride and chit,
turning Love into an old woman beggar.

Down at the well she lowered the bucket
of her soul and asked,
"How long until I drink the waters of Thee?"
But this thirst did not converse with its own echo.

Guru

Hero of humanity,
you are the lighthouse for wayward ships
who have tossed about on the waves of disquiet
over a savage sea.

Lionhearted among men,
White knight in shining armor of wisdom,
you rescue the maiden of
Purity in our hearts.

Ten thousand internal cries
          find solace
in the wellspring of your words.

Over our barren desert spirits
you make flow fountains of prosperity.
Those once dry sands produce the everlasting
bloom of fertility.

Healer of mortality
Panacea for mankind
Remedy for restlessness
We come to you: weak, weary
  battered, broken
  sickened, selfish
  dispirited, deluded
  fearful, frantic
  insecure, insatiable
  unfinished, unbelieving
  hapless, homeless
  neurotic, nauseous
    naked!
Who but you turns not away
from our mortal strife?

Who but you has the transcendental vision
to enter the dark cave of the animal,
and bring forth the Gems of Divinity.

Fear

You. I have grown tired of your tyranny.
You. In your small house
with no windows
and too many locks!

Spreading disquiet wherever you go,
like an itchy rash
that begs to be scratched.

A sorcerer of foul play;
Foul because you stink
of death and dread
Play because you turn men
into frozen puppets.

Lurking in the graveyard of doubt,
        unclean phantasm
        walking menace in the mind
whispering all the time "defeat, defeat."

How many swim into your net
and suffocate on the soiled decks
of your pirate ship?
Fiendish Fisherman!

What can you offer to desperate humanity?
Enslavement won't do

for we are all creatures
of flight.

Just as the eagle feels not the burden
of weight,

You too will be forgotten
as we soar beyond your boundaries.

Breath

You come in and out
to tell me who I am,
but I don't hear you.

Bridging all rivers
with the ocean,
you fan the fire of the world.

Your ways are the waves
that roll upon shore,
later inhaled by the lungs of the sea.

In quiet humility
you enter our house
whispering of something else.

Incessantly chanting
the song of Time
and Eternity; of Him and me.

You are the string
which ever joins
the pearls of Life.

A thankless necessity
to preserve our presence,
so that we may listen.

If I Meet You

If I meet you
as a beggar
will you scorn
my poverty

If I meet you
as a king
will you laugh
at my ornamentation

If I meet you
as a friend
will you disapprove
my familiarity

If I meet you
as a scholar
will you reproach
my understanding

If I meet you
as my beloved
will you hide
your face of wrath?

The Sapera's Song

Lightness, bear us up
so we can fully show
Love is working her miracle here.

Into the mix of sugar and milk,
one will stay white- the other will fade.

The student asks, "Are we building up
or tearing down? I brought my cup
and want a taste."

The teacher's reply, "Just find your tension
then let it go. Turn your cup the other way."

Oh Heart, we were both drunk
with foolish notions
but in this darkness anyone
will do.

You hide a gain in your
tight, clinched sinews,
changing unwilling as
others have changed.

But when the teacher appears
with his sapera's song,
Something awakes, uncoils and rises up
from this basket we call earth.

Yes

The minute I call out

YES to you,

All the countless hours

of maybe

will step aside

that I may see you

in that YES!

River Song

There is a river which flows
through the channels of my mind,
and glistens the surface
of my sun-colored heart.

Beyond the hollow silhouettes
which fuse together to form
the shadows of night,
this river dances past what is still.

Holding the secrets of life
in her silent interior,
it fills the twisted spaces
with a natural rhythm.

Ripples whisper hush
as they break on the bank,
And every living thing seems to sing
a hymn to the sun.

The Dream

Waves course through
the channels of space
arousing the quiescence
of dreamless sleep.

Surging with motion
they spread with a current
filling the shadows
with radiant light.

Gossamer ribbons stream
into color
and dance in the spectrum
of virtual sight.

Shaping the image
of ideas reflected,
gathering myths
from the mind of the dream.

A Fist Full of Chickpeas

little bird fears to flee
from its golden cage.

monkey is betrayed
by a fist full of chickpeas.

the worm in his mud pit
declines a palace guide,
and the dog draws his own blood
sucking on a bone.

a master tries to pry the soul free
in so many ways.

mine takes his students, like a bunch
of old proverbs, and awakens them
to open bounty, a way out of narrow jars,
a path and map to a kingdom

And provides real meat we can
sink our teeth into
until these impressions coalesce.

Flower of Compassion

When you feel the sharp
sting of the world
from the wasp of desire
never fulfilled,

I will come to you then
as the balm of kindness
and soothe the burn
of broken dreams.

When the fading
rose of pleasure
withers upon the many
thorns of pain,

I will come to you then
as the flower of compassion
and emit the perennial
perfume of joy.

When calamity lays siege
to the foundation
of your being
and leaves you in stony ruins,

I will come to you then
as the shelter of friendship
and surround you with doors
opening to the sky.

The Disciple

I am a disciple.
I carry the fuel
for sacred fire
and walk towards the
Bridge Supreme.

Long I have sat
at the feet of the world
and made the songs
of olden times
my refuge.

It is for that reason I sing
in the midst of struggle
and struggle
while others sing.

I am a lover
of what is hidden
yet I chase not after ghosts
but pursue with reason
what is living.

Living in me
is the mystic light
which illumines
the path of sacred duty
and noble aspiration.

I follow the words
of the Guru
who reveals the mystery
of Vedanta through the grace
of pure vision.

Some may say,
"there is my daughter"
"there is my wife"
but in Truth I am
a blooming lily on the waters of life.

I follow in the footsteps
of those before me
who crossed the river of fear
and obtained vision
through harmony of Yoga.

From that sorrowless shore,
the lovers of Brahman
shine with victory
and kindle devotion
in the hearts of the many.

Led from the unreal to the real
I, too, will cross the
Bridge Supreme
and stream down, like mountain rain
into the One.

In the Range of Fire

Friend, these stained glass windows
let in the light-
your perception is not so different.

Listen, there is nothing speaking here
no Tower of Babel
no church bell chimes
only this alliance you sought out
because everything you want will find you
eventually.

I can hear what you won't say.
In this fierce world where mindless habit
spreads like a cancer over originality.

Don't pretend. Don't begin a barrage of
"I'm fines"
when the lantern of our hearts shares
the same light,
and the same lamp black.

This riddle of me solves you;
and so it is from a deep affection
that I say Come,
stand in the range of fire.
Lift up the blindfold and see
you are surrounded by centuries
of invitation.

Hourglass

Since all contrivance sprang
from a tail in an open mouth,
let me uncoil the toil of words
and say whatever surfaces
from the quicksands of the soul.

Lord, I am overturned
with praying and preying;
for these passions of mind to heart
form our inner hourglass.

My love within has become as lost
as a caravan of countless sands.
Between each bowl, my soul ever shifts
like battered winds across barren land.

Throughout the life, I have only known
brief interruptions from a sorrowful storm.
And so it is with a passionate ache
that I invoke your presence!

For when my Christ comes,
this glass will not measure
Up to the diamonds that come
through his glance.

But for now, what cravings
run and blow and relentlessly roll
down this funnel-my unknown Self!

Banyan

Immanent tree, you stand
in the center
of the many offshoots
which emanate from your boundless mind.

Walking, you are ever still
to witness the tangled outgrowths
mingle together
as the fruits of your design.

Is there no end to your reach,
where upon newness is forever born
and suspended by the fertile
touch of your outstretched limbs?

Dangling in the twisted jungle
of your moving mosaic,
all are only offspring
from your potent seed.

All arms extend in
wishful imitation
to yoke the meshes
of your braided maze.

Aerial roots made solid only
by bending downward
to touch the mighty dust
of your well planted feet.

The Sleeper

All is a dream
in the mind of the dreamer,
and I am that sleeper
who wakes from the dream.

Through countless reflections
I see what is seeming,
then peer beyond reason
and reach the Supreme.

The sleeper gives substance
to schemes of the spirit,
then watches the dreaming
from distance serene.

I am that dreamer
who imagines my being
in the realm of existence,
though sleeping I seem.

The Shadow

I have journeyed so,
like a weary pilgrim,
over many winding paths
on dim and dusty roads.

Turning my back to the sun
I, like a fool,
followed the shadow
which was my own.

Lured by desire
to capture a phantom,
I stumbled unknowing
away from my home.

'Twas maddened obsession
which kept me pursuing
in any direction
this shadow did roll.

To taunt my misgivings
the earth she kept turning,
setting her shades
apart from the sun.

Roaming through countries
by misguided reason,
my homeland was lost
in direction unknown.

Alone with the landscape
I sat and lamented
over empty endeavors
and unsure return.

Casting its figure
in front of my footsteps,
this shadow did mock
that I followed its lead.

The sting of that truth
stood ahead of me blazing;
so I turned to abandon
the shadow behind.

Leading the way
eclipsing the shader,
on well lighted roads
I walked towards the sun.

Substance

I set out to find myself,
and saw the dust
which was my bones
blow across the desert sands.

I set out to find myself,
and felt the waters leak
from all my gates
and flood the open ground.

I set out to find myself,
but fire consumed
the blaze of my eyes
and I saw no more.

I set out to find myself,
yet I was lost
in the airy spaces
between what moved.

I set out to find myself
in the ethereal sea,
and found I had vanished
from the substance of me.

Two Ways

Two are the ways
to govern the mind;
two are the fruits
those actions do bind.

One is the path
which inclines toward pleasure;
the sensual life
of unwilling measure.

One is the path
which embraces the good;
through disciplined purpose
of Nature understood.

Prudence

Reason be thy touchstone
for thought, word and deed-
there be surest counsel
that be wisdom's creed.

Consider how the wise
discriminate each fruit,
counting not the leaves
they penetrate the root.

The mind who takes his counsel
from imprudent, frenzied thought
seeks its own destruction
from all that it has sought.

But if with keen discernment
results are clearly weighed,
Prudence be thy glory
and folly feels her blade.

Mother, It Is Thy Mercy

Mother, it is thy mercy
which melts the hearts of men
and makes us feel like little children
beside your lotus feet.

We have been playing
in your flower gardens
for too long a season,
as fascination took us far.

Like butterflies, we fluttered
from colored petal to color
and heard not you
calling us home.

In heeding not for want of mirth,
we tarried beyond our stay.
Wandering through your garden great,
we tangled in the vines.

Oh Mother, amidst the ivy
not knowing it would sting;
and thistle weed has torn our dress
in which you made with care.

Our soiled clothes and dirty hands
do show of mischief spent;
which burdens us with guilt
as we approach thy cottage door.

Yet unable to forgive ourselves
for committing vain misdeeds,
we prepared to see thy wrath
await the threshold door.

But pardon filled thy eyes,
kindness thy embrace,
and we did melt beneath that mercy
as love our shame erased.

Looking Beyond

Lord, in desperation
I struggle to uncover
my own hidden talent,
only to reveal some semblance of you
in me
some clue to prove you dwell in
me too.
As a grain of your glory can sustain the
weight of the sea.

Let me not forget, to always
look beyond
what is lost and what is found.

For if I am master
of any purpose this world has
but see not you behind all skills,
then I have failed in full
at the beginning of my endeavor.
And I have lost already
what I will gain
in the crumbling sands
of change.

How Can It Be

How can it be, my Lord
that you remember me
within every thought
I forget about you?

How can it be, my God
that you remember me
as my breath I use
to run from you?

How can it be, True Love
that you remember me
in my heart which beats
tight and hard?

How can it be, Oh One
that you remember me
when enmeshed in the many
I remember you not!

In Many a Crusading Hour

In many a crusading hour,
I have tossed and turned
like one who is restless
in the hours of rest.

Times when sweet repose
did not heed my command
but left me alone
with the midnight hours of my mind.

Vain moments when the moon
took all that is earthly
and sent out her beams
to seize the sun.

Hours when full circles
were not quite complete and I
was obliged to keep
my pack with the night.

Under Fortune's skies
the stars seemed to burn
a steel wall of NOT YET
into my dreams.

Yes, wild nights did visit me often
during my life's campaign.
And frenzied howls did sound, through the blackness
without a witness, into the night!

Unhidden

I am unhidden from thee,
vulnerable and exposed.
Like naked winter trees
I have no leaves in which to hide.

The clever guise of words and face fools not you,
Oh Penetrating Light!
As even thoughts belie themselves
by subtle mutation in silence divide.

Deeds in the breeze
blow quickly past
through screaming, scheming canyons;
leaving only stony intention intact.

With ease you unearth
my interior core,
casting the rest
in a dusty, hollow heap.

I lay bare my open plains
beneath the eyes of the sky
and shake with a wildflower or two,
before they vanish under the snow.

In the fields of vision
you trace down each blade of grass
before it breaks dirt,
and establish your seeing inside the earth.

The Myth of Man

Perhaps man is just a rumor
whispered amongst the Gods,
who revolve through constellations to make up fabrica-
tions!

Perhaps man is a myth,
a fairy tale told by non-believers
where our silly self-existence
comes from tongues spinning fiction.

Can you imagine man's stubborn reality stepping aside
to play the part of a celestial sport, where his entire
saga shrinks to an anecdote set by a star?

Man, Oh Man

Man, Oh Man you laugh
when you should weep
well, I will share
your unshed tears.

Man, Oh Man your confusion
runs deep
but I will wear my losses
as gain.

Man, Oh Man in your conscious
does creep
every thought of mine
is yours just the same.

Goodbye

I have said goodbye
more than I wished
as the waving hands of change
always seem to bid farewell.

Like a seafaring drifter
blown between islands,
I've moved through the shifts
of beginning and end.

And always with a sense
of untimely measure
did the close of glad days
seize me by surprise.

Why in the midst
of comfortable familiars
the future pushed the present
out of established ways?

Why does goodbye
fill every newness
as the severing split
within every seed?

Goodbye seems to sit
as my one sole companion,
alone in the sea
of dispersing waves.

And yet she assures me
upon our departure,
her sails catch the winds
to newborn chance lands.

Him

They say that His joy
sustains all the worlds
and within just a fraction
of that joy we live.

They say that behind
the curtain of life
He exists in the heart
as awakening flame.

They say that of greatness
His is the highest
in a country where knowledge
and knower are one.

They say that of Gods
you may never find Him
but open the eye
and He you become.

My Dreams

My dreams never learned
to unfurl their wings
and fly to the heights
in which they had aimed.

My dreams never learned
to break through the shell
and shake off the casing
within which they laid.

My dreams were afraid
to flee from their nest
as their faith, being frail
expected a fall.

Yes, my dreams
never learned to
unfurl their wings

until now.

Divided Nation

The enemy is not God,
but ignorance
which destroys us
again and again.

As long as the Spirit
stays locked in the narrow chambers
of a partitioned heart,

As long as the Truth
is buried below
the black ash of decay,

As long as the One
appears broken apart
by the rotating turns of the two,

no country shall keep
no eye will not weep
no freedom be won
no tie not undone
no land without stain
no body not pained

and there will be no rest.
and there will be no rest.

The Third Day

Lord, my altar is strewn
with bread and wine
for the dialogue of the heart.

On high my heavenly host suspends,
in its golden pyx out of a dove.
Love, lift these wings out of the fire
for a soul surfaces through the burn of The Son.

What else can we conjure up
but our own pain wanting back;
To its nest in this cathedral
on a bridge between the eyes
where the wind tunnels cross.

Lord, when all food flies back to your hunger
and Life finds its silent but speaking tongue,
then I will live the mystery of my heart's dialogue.
Shedding my linens
on the third day saying,

"Ours is not the body of Christ
apart from consciousness,
But the empty sepulchre, the removed stone,
The man formed in light-resurrected."

Unity

I am the self-same
symbol as you.
We make one word which
whispers our name
then breathes our joys and sorrows
into the wind.

When the wheel rolls,
we are the spokes
placed in the center of
rotation and spin.
I am the self-same
circle as you.

Together we burn
in the spirit of life,
like the dancing flames
within one waving light.
I am the self-same
fire as you.

The substance of us
is woven like thread,
from every beginning
until every end,
I am in self-same
union with you.

Spirit

make us know Spirit
in knowing Spirit
one knows all
not for knowing all
but for knowing all as Spirit
which fills us with wonder
and captures our devotion unceasing
in that state
through such devotion
we are vindicated from our sins
and shine in duty evermore
to that Spirit
once we know.

Offering

I came to your altar, my Lord
and watched the devotees
bring flowers and incense;
I watched as they brought
excellent gifts.
But I have no excellent gift
to place on your altar,
not of sparkle or shine.
I brought only the spoiled fruits
and rusted chains
which I alone have cherished,
for too long.

Butterfly Spirit

What moves when I am still
and is still when I move?
This butterfly spirit alights where it will
and alludes the capture of grasping hands.

It flutters through wandering
winds of the mind
and rests on the open
petals of peace.

Its wings are of shadow and light;
Within its nature lives the
riddle of change.

In some it crawls like forgotten power-
In some it flies as glorious play-

Upon what strange prison
sets its captive free?
In newness appearing
though immersed in the same.

Butterfly Spirit smiles in the creature
who walks over grass,
without any wings.

Great is the Man

Great is the God
who apprehends all things,
Great is the man
who apprehends the God.
For all of his life
is lit with a beauty
and all of his acts
are anchored in prayer.

For him, all the forms
are filled with the Spirit
worthy of honor,
worthy of praise.

He speaks to the earth
within every moment
and delights in the knowledge
of listening ear.

Great is the God
who apprehends all things,
Great is the man
who apprehends the God.
In the joy of pure vision
he sees through the nothing,
his tears of devotion
nourish the world.

The Inner Mystic

The inner mystic is witness
to the retelling wheel
and all who migrate
across the secular skies.

While countless deaths stack
upon my soul, and distant
memories seep into my mind
drop by drop...

Thinking them new, I
relive the tolls paid to life
within the unrevealed grooves
of a reminding dream.

How many moments
did I repeat
the same, unlearned song
and mistake it for something new?

Did destiny mask my
future moves
and save my tomorrow
from remains of today?

Woeful habits confined in conditions,
the ceremonies of birth and death
together find meaning
by walking in the wake of each others steps.

Behind them lingers
an ancient wisdom
like a recollection of sweet perfume,
whose scent is felt by heart and mind.

Stirring thoughts of transcending sorts
echo in the caverns within my range,
like something urgent
but far away.

Dripping nectar in measured portion,
the inner mystic waits in greatness
and prepares the day
to deluge my soul.

Vedanta

Vedanta reveals
supreme revelation
through knowledge affirmed
with a veritable seal.

Experience transforms
the wise with assurance
that man, in his search,
can find his true joy.

At which precise moment
the mind is absorbed
and comprehension changed
to a thing absolute?

None but Purusha
who dwells in himself
can witness the flowers
which grow from his seed.

Impelled by the knower
to crystallize reason,
the truth of the Vedas
is clearly perceived.

Tending the Fire

Since the voice first stirred
through the many waters,
it rippled into words
on a churning sea.

A solitary sound
swimming through the void
called to the living,
"tend my fire."

From out of the friction
of words on the waters,
a fire was kindled
under the waves.

Shinning like lightening
in every direction,
this fire reflected
the soul of the world.

Within every life
its power was feeding;
while breathing expression
in what burned to live.

From ancient times
it opened man's eyes
and built its temple
inside of the dark.

With spirited force
it spread through creation,
shooting out sparks
aglow from the source.

Sustained by the touch
of quickening impulse,
lit animation
fueled definite aim.

And thus flashed oblation
enveloped in beings,
tending the fire's
encompassing flames.

Surface Trade

I used to see newness emerging
from every corner and think
Ah, how great to acquaint
with that which is new.

Fresh in the medley
of unripe beginnings,
my taste was for fruits
unseasonably green.

In the birth of each second
cries the curious now,
surrounded with appeal
of wealth to obtain.

As if this newness,
an insecure thing,
vies for attention
like a self-conscious maid.

She stands uncommon
with novel promise,
and we in courting
open the doors.

Outward she spreads,
external we tread,
letting invention
clutter our drawers.

In the study of recent
newfangled gloss,
lives the unseen death
of a precious old.

After years of surface trade,
I've seen the golden idol modern
sink into the common
beneath its own weight.

As a drink that is touched
by shallow cup
repeats the same toast
of frivolous gain.

Nay to the latest,
matured, now I say
give me the ancient
interior gaze.

One Turn

When one exhalation
awakens Nature
from the narrow chambers
of her cradle grave,

When all the still
is blown to storm
and image begins
its whirlwind charade,

When man sees the first
glimpse of himself
in the distant source
from which he sprang,

When evolution waits
to complete a rotation
and sits in the middle
of half a breath;

When drawing inhalation
pulls back creation
into the mighty portal
of vanished, vacant sleep,

When all independence
recoils back
and conditions dissolve
in absolute fear,

When man in his smallness
shrinks to a memory
and enters the cause
of regenerate reel,

When effects spiral backwards
and restless expression
surrenders itself
to suspended embrace,

Then did one turn
account for the ages
spread into currents
of life, force and death-

When once the Great God has taken a breath.
When once the Great God has taken a breath.

Wishing Well

With the last penny
Fortune could afford
me in my disgust
for the mundane,
I stood at the edge
of the well and smelt
the deep, cold dirt of earth
which had the odor
of solid promise.

Drawing up my cherished wish,
I poured the vessel
of my heart
and spoke my hope
to the nobody coin.
As if fate would honor this
meager gift,
or chance would change
or rearrange
or if magic granted
secret deals.

But enchanted by
a lingering hint,
I weighed the simple
wonder of If-
The fragile dreams
sustained by myth,
The well for filling
wishes with,
And tossed my charm
into the pit.

Release

I don't know why, but this
warden of a world tries
to keep me small
keep me uncertain
keep me.

And when I bang my tight, white
fists on his swelling chest,
I hear the drumming laughter
which makes him dance.

And when I cry, I see
the salt of my tears
fall to his plate to spice his food!

Well, I have tricks too.
I have been plotting during
my sentence of solitary dim.
TONIGHT I will play
like one who is dead
then flee, like a ghost
from his clutches of steel.

Word Sculpture

I like a sculpture which

points a piercing limb out

across the separate

sea of ego

and touches upon the vulnerable,

secret pulse

of a gathered humanity

in the one listening mind

under the waves.

The Impeller

I am filled with gladdened wonder
when I look about
and see the splendid beauty
of your ineffable ways.

It is even more
that I do not see all,
but only a fraction because
of my small receiving self.

The outpour of enduring rejoice
spans throughout the ages,
with its ancient, new
loving embrace.

Forever we come
and drink from your cup,
forever you pour
the drink of yourself!

No Words

In my gut I know what's right
and though I press upon my pen,
I can't put words on inward light
though write, I must and try again.

You pressed on me an indelible mark
in ink you wrote my every page,
and though my heart caught smallest spark
its flames of love brought fires rage.

In taste of salt when soul does stir;
In place of heat when heart does melt;
In these I fail to write what's sure,
When devotion speaks, no words are felt.

The Smallest Fraction

I see how you remake yourself
in all the souls who surface in time.
I know it is you who portions devotion
in all the men and even me,
for you alone write adoration's lines.
And though I know the
smallest fraction,
I swear, in that share
could I forever live.

Under the Almond Tree

To draw us in, it comes and goes.

In the silence of contrivance,
the boatman rows.

Far be it for me, to navigate this tree.
Or to make my heart-the resurrection fern-
return to the glorious shores of The Self.

But if Duty be the spring out of rock, priest and king
then let us evolve in our own natural way,
And ask what was made for the asking:

A life of expansion and compassionate action;

One in which we forget not our ancestors, nor the gods
Nor our duty to teacher and God.
To be a divine healer for each other,
but first and foremost heal our Selves.

In that way, may we have our work,
relinquishing the fruits,
with an object of attaining the goal of human birth.

And when we ask, for the asking
it goes and it comes
saying, "Forget the little bliss, Love has a plan
Its branches drip with a sweeter ecstasy,

I am the blossom, the chosen staff
and you all- like bewildered Princes
standing in the shade
under Aaron's almond tree."

What Fears

What fears can send

their tempest force-

to me a disrespectful gale,

which puffs its cheeks

to blow off course

the ship that needs no wind to sail.

Inconsequential Things

Give me your heart
and let me speak frank,
as flattery serves only
to keep you a slave.

Enough gathering of autumn's leaves.
Enough embrace of disintegrating earth.

You will see, enough is never enough;
and hollowed reeds should not be filled,
lest they seal and play no song.

Why stay imprisoned in the
stubborn definition of what you
believe you need
and need to be?

Be not an iceberg holding hard its form
who finds no rest upon the sea,
but melt in the waters
which gave you your form.

True, you must renounce
and walk through the empty
where neither pleasure nor goodness dwell.

But you cannot postpone the rising sun
nor tell the night to walk in day.
When the arrow is shot into your breast,
be sure that the falcon is circling down.

The King will reclaim you
from the wild, the sorrow
and the hollow
know this to be, in Truth, for the good.

Think how this possession
of "my's" and "I's"
steals from you the Truth of
"Thou art That?"

And though you may choose
to not let go, in the end
even your borrowed hands
will mingle with the ash.

Enough staking claim
to a mountain of dust!
Enough of this clinging
to one dirty bead!

You wield the power
behind every atom;
Why do you work
for inconsequential things?

The Desert Must Be Known

The desert must be known
by those who wish to reach the sea,
so do not deny desolation
its own rightful place.

Though no sense of pleasures found
nor do angels flash their wings,
every paragon of realization
walked his share of barren lands.

In truth, the very thought of desert
keeps devotees from their quest,
and so they sip from shore-bound shells
to fill the thirst of an ocean's heart.

Along death's valley you will see
the necessity of frozen fire;
and how one touch by inner flair
quells the burn of life's desire.

Pass beyond the fear of naught,
Let no doubt there cause retreat,
and though you thirst for this or that-
know this empty, too, is Divine Grace.

Lack and loss refine and carve
channels for the ocean surge.
Meet the sea of boundless shores
walk the vacant desert sands.

Beyond and Beyond, listen clear
you will hear the wise rejoice.
For every step on this abandoned land
sounds the drums of victory!

Life

Life-what not lives in your circle
of benediction?

Lift up our hearts to your
center of awareness
where all spokes stem from your
willingness to be.

Let us live straight, as we are your
flaming arrows soaring
towards the waters of cool, still
Mountain Lake.

May your power increase noble aim
so with genuine spirit we serve you true
like the rays of the sun, by kindness
multiply your name.

We, of the moon, stream down in rain
and wait for your vital hands
to lift us up
lift us in
lift us to the great distance which waits
near.

Let us feed life with Life
Think of life with Life
Speak of life with Life
Live of life with Life

With all our combined endeavors and grace
let us forever prostrate to the
precious opportunity
at the feet of Life.

Carry on, sail towards the dawn.
Carry on, your wings bear our worth.

The One Waits

Behind what you think-
Behind what you know-
The One is waiting
in the eye of the hurricane.

If you pass the walls of storm-
If your fix gives not to twist-
Then reach into the wind
without hand;
walk across the wall, but don't swagger.

Shed the hope for lightning's flash
and let what you are become lost.

Like surface sands on a windy beach,
erase the footprints in your mind.

Under the rough rampage
He calls with the voice
of an indigo ocean,
from the depths of a peace
cushioned in blue.

Far from the violent, the rage
and the clash-
Far from foam that rolls and breaks
into the hissing background of crashing roar.

Farther still, from the nothing worm
which day by day
makes its meal of you.

Be not a willing participant
to your own grave.
Pick not the daisies to lay
at your tomb.
Enter not the cyclone, the wheel,
the cage.

The One waits for you
to cast off!
To say one final sound
in that terrible, auspicious hour
when you, in living surrender, withdraw your rays
like a setting sun and shine
in the source of concentrated light.

Where still is the harbor
and Surya reigns as a jewel in the storm.

Crossroads

One thousand grave mistakes
gather power, from the anger
and the ugly
which distance does show.

And I sit between
blood and gain,
and feel no claim
to triumph or defeat.

The road splits me
like a knife, night and day
and I fear my strain
may stretch no more.

That on this road of dusty straits
I, to my last breath
fade and give way-
laying on the path of half a nothing.

But the middle is trouble
more than I can bear,
as an ancient battle silently rages
upon my fields, war is waged.

Clashing stars set me at
dual-purpose,
and upon that sharp crux
my way is harsh and obscure.

Corners come at every cross,
and choiceless choices
present only one way
in which to walk the razor's edge.

The compass points its arrows
down a place I still disdain;
and yet from all directions
I hear a solemn dirge.

Neither sit nor lay me down
upon the crossing roads.
Come, my strength, child of failings
turn your temper inward saved.

We know not to tarry
on two branching walks,
these trembles cannot stumble
through another rising sun.

Evolution

I became a distant place,
then set out to advance across the divide.
Small pieces of me pass and loose their worth
as I rush on and reach for Thee.

From the depths of a place
maddened with fearful joy,
my soul awakes
and seeks for its own.

No senseless, restless surface
can keep me from the One
who remains the same within and without
my own True Self!

I am here amongst you now,
but a deathless voice conjures me
to rise and become the extent-
and it is only natural that I go.

By Grace

By the wings of Grace we lift up our hearts
to the Lord.

It is of humble certainty
She cannot be won
She cannot be caught
She cannot be held
But by the mystery of Grace alone,
She moves among men.
She moves of her own accord
and chooses when and where to alight.
She is the bee by whose nectar all becomes sweet.

By Grace, this city is kept alive.
By Grace, this life becomes a city.
She allows us to run far away,
and She pulls the net which draws us back.

She protects men from calamity
and sometimes disguises in the face of despair.
Ever guiding men in the field of action.
Ever is the prompter of our prayers,
our progress,
our future gains.

Grace does not work by action,
but action works by the power of Grace.
Grace gives unmerited assistance-
Man cannot say, "I did that"
if he remembers what removed his troubles
and set him up high.

Grace pulls one out of the whirlpool
of action and reaction,
yet no force or will or command can grant
what Grace won't give.

Self-sacrifice, humanity, vision
come from her hand.
As even these lines I could not write,
if not for her lending harmony
to my baffled brain.

She is a pristine place
where none can go-
none can rush her doors, charge her gate.
Only She can come to us
and once kissed by her lips,
hardness fades away.

Grace descends upon the lost,
the lonely.
Grace makes a lion out of a man.

When with Grace, obstacles disintegrate
and any way is easy to reach.
Grace makes heroes out of the afraid.
Grace appoints kings who rule by charm.
Grace is the bird of paradise who comes to our tree.

Grace is above men's thought
yet she guides the mind in subtle ways,
therefore it is right to give thanks
to the power behind the good which we think we do.

Grace gives to man liberation.
Grace is the Lord's abundance of love.
No one is ever worthy to receive her,
but a heart of compassion invites her to stay.

As the setting sun startles the water
with its silent beauty, Grace comes to man
to lift him to love...

under that sanction
all will be healed.

The Cosmic Echo

The One Love became many
and that many serve the One.

The Lord of singular consciousness
calls upon himself as "we"
for his fullness divided,
but did not decrease.

He is the reservoir of all virtues
and his qualities pervade the world.
Just as blood circulates in the body,
He exists as the fluid of life
causing the heart of Nature to beat.

He is a cell unto himself, a secret chamber,
with one pulsing word
which dances in the light and shadow of itself.
Like a fire that burns in a snow-capped cave,
He vanquishes dark fear with his light
and melts all hearts encased in vice.

He portioned himself amongst the deities,
the demons and man
as a symbol of good, evil and struggle.
He is the highest of his own hierarchy!

Man is dear to Him who is dear
because he wanders in this vast universe
and says in sadness, "I am a mystery unto myself."

Thinking such, he searches.
In searching, he asks, "Who am I,
surely not this pleasure nor this pain
under that power, I die every day?"

In the immortality of His own idea,
Where the Gods assist receptive minds,
In the wish-fulfilling awareness
of His own question asked,
He answers the cosmic echo, "I am amen with no
end."

Heart's Desire

I have not risen above these desires
but one desire is to be rid of the rest.

We suffer the agony of expectation
and the anger of discontent.
We exist, but do not live-
like caged birds who sing for their master
and not the rising sun.

Today deals in prostitution
from yesterdays indiscretion
and tomorrows wanton glance.

As Nature draws again and again
the heavy heart of steely desire
back to the earthly furnace
where fire forges passion's blade.

Why, my friend, should you and I
be victims of such device?

We are compelled by fear
and lack of faith;
yet even if we pried open the fists of this earth
and held all the accomplishment therein,
would we still not want for space?

I, too, wish to attain success
but it is no measure of character
to love that which is cruel.

We stand at the frontier
beyond the limits of eager men.
A vulture circles,
anxious in his stark sky-
his hunger would have us dead
our hunger would have us die.

You and I have much in common,
we are uncommon subjects
to a common flaw:
We suffer the seldom glimpse
of gratification in a world
dominated by duality.

I have not risen above these desires,
but one desire is to be rid of the rest.
We shall let that one be the
foremost speaker,
until the weight of its honor
is anchored in peace.

What is most dear to all hearts
is the one paramount desire
which, when realized, encompasses all that is valued
as it folds in upon itself.

It is the star of absolute magnitude
who surrenders its light
into the center of
consummate love.

Rusted Nail

In day comes everyone's turn
	to try.

We wake fresh and glisten with the hope of
	Again.

The ghost was never real
but its thick mist makes us forget
as we slip into delirium
of a distorted façade.

Until we rust from the weather
of too many blows
and the hammer hits
splintered wood,

Until we are driven, like a stubborn nail
by the forceful strike
of a stable hand,

Night swallows our existence-
and in blackness we
crouch and wait.

Something Less Vulnerable

I make no record of chosen words
but speak without guile, from the heart.
It is only in the silence of sincere dialogue
a man can offer the best of himself.
Anyway, why should I hide, you know my intent!

Let us leave reason and religion
out of this conversation,
I think they cage the wild heart.

Love wants to flap and sing
and make itself a fool,
because it is free and fearless.

Every mortal is born a seeker
seeking his own immortality.
The fact that he seeks proves he already knows
something better than what he sees.

He turns over so many rocks
and even musters the strength
to turn mountains on their tops, or die trying.
Rather than remember, he continues to forget
and one must work hard and sweat to forget.

The world moves in his thoughts,
and he moves after the world.
He is on a treadmill
pacing his steps to the speed of desire.
Things are in motion-to stop in a sudden is to fall.
Momentum is master now.

See us-diseased by wayward will,
lost to defining the world
with a false notion of significant needs.

We have withered on our own frail stem
and sold our fragrance to the breeze.

I really don't wish to measure meaning,
but Lord, you are in the center of this
great, perfect, endless circle
which at once is terror and joy
which at once drives men mad and sets them free.

We are but your stars, awake and asleep,
in orbit around your might.

My downright prayer for all I see
is that we may come to rest in the
kindest of joy and
become, once again,
something less vulnerable.

Chant

The universe is dancing
to the name of the Lord.
In that one word
lives the sound of infinite creation.

It is the cosmic song
serenading the ear of the world,
which weaves harmony
into this vast quilt of life.

Chant the holy name
and your conscious will dive
into a channel of the deepest mantra-
then you will willingly get lost.

Fly, like a love-struck songbird
and we will meet in the chords
of the ocean's crest,
as diamond daughters of the dawn.

I tell you, I have dipped the tips of my wings
into a sea of devotion
and soared in the roar
of its silver-tongued tune.

So it is Lord, your name became a great wave
and I, a glad bird, ready to sail
a heart-swell of music
upon its one winded rail.

Forever Full

So many snowflakes fall
to cover a mountain.
And you, like one so unique,
glide down in your short span of glory.
Rays of light shine through delicate glass ice
and display your complexity.

In the still wilderness,
you look out from your
frosted window of water
and believe the pattern
is something complete.

You want to offer fullness to what is forever full
but your diamond is borrowed moonlight
frozen in the night sky.
You came from the place you are going,
and that beauty you carry is the delight
of another summit.

You came, without a sound,
in your laced veil, to cover a mountain.
But like all the others
who fell to the mountain's feet,
you silently shed the weight of design
and melted in the knowledge
of what always was.

Asana

Eight million beings wait
to take form in me,
when I move my Self
through this dance.

Then I know why you have virtue,
and how to borrow
your given strength.

I know what lends comfort
to living so simple,
and watch as you remain
still and true.

When I try to bend like you,
I begin to understand that
all must bend,
all must reach beyond themselves.

In this thought of me, many pass through
and many linger-
like incense in a holy place.

This body has the capacity
to be filled with such states.
This body can hold
that peaceful perfume.

As one steady channel
I find ease in my being
and balance in the center
where the many are me.

Eight million beings wait
to take form
because love in The One
could not be contained.

They surface through the lonely
island of my being
and embrace my spirit
so I stand not apart.

Taking the shape of my nomadic mind
to remind me of the latent
living in me.

Then I know the secret of
sun salutation-
when I move my Self
through this dance.

And I am renewed
in the joy of becoming.
And I am renewed
in the joy of joining the same.

Revelation

I will return-
because nothing is wasted of me.

It is written in my heart
but you give life to my words,
You are the Soul of my words,
which would otherwise decay
like lingering ashes
without a fire.

My hope is born in the wish
that you will return-
because nothing is wasted in Thee.

My thirsty inward ears await
your lightening voice,
pregnant beyond the birth of words.

In stillness you command such power
over my restless mind,
you overtake my every step.
I cannot move
I cannot keep
I cannot blow one straw
with all the wind which reigns in storm,
my tempest tamed before your might-
and I will not, nor draw a breath.

In an instant you bestow sight
for which my whole life I
could not see.
My eyes, I could close and look no more.
My tongue, I could fold behind closed lips.

You make known the question
which burns in all of our hearts,
it is the yearning behind
searching returns.

We are yours to reveal,
and you belong to your own
forgotten self
who needs to glimpse
the curve of its face
to remember what is real.

As for me, I wade in the river
feeling its force push against my stance.
Evolution turns and returns
in my rippled reflection-
while the waters of revelation
curl at my feet.

The Dragon's Lair

Perhaps you thought I could be outlined in your idea
Perhaps you should look again,
my ocean is deeper.

Perhaps you thought you could always find your way
Perhaps you should seek again,
my ocean is wider.

You never saw this path
and fear to call it mine.
My world does not sit or stand
in the creases of your palm,
nor in the mind's savage language.

The ones I have served
will have to be sufficient
it is all, and it is enough.

That which is unwilling and helpless
I called upon to give life,
yet I deliver every one of you.
I am guardian
of the sleeping serpent in your spine.

My words are blood
and they are spilling now...
Into every heart my words speak
beyond the beat which keeps the soul.

You know not this battlefield
in which I play.
I will slay that which thinks of me,
for I am not found by thought.
I will slay that which thinks of me not,
for I am the one promise you want to keep.

I have gone into your secret place
and placed a dragon at its gate.
Before this treasure I entreat you to claim,
do you not see me breathing the flames?

Soul (Jiva)

Soul, my Soul
how many faces have
called you their own?
From how many eyes
have you shined your light?

Oh, my Soul, I cannot
trace your steps
through rain, in earth
from plant, man or beast
Your lineage frightens my mind!

My reason is possessed
by the transient manifest
and I search for the subtle
but with eyes, I don't see.

Will you not enter
into my perception
least I cling
to what will betray me?

Immersed in this ocean
I thirst for a drop
yet my heart is a house
surrounded by fire.

Come out of this flaming house
spill yourself upon my
blind hunger
that I may have victory!

Then I will change like water
to wine
and Death, in his drunkenness
will find me not.

Grit

I have been shaken
and sifted so-
the sands of my soul run out
your world sieve.

Did you shape that
peculiar expression
on earth's face,
One of pity and hate?

For she nurtures men
with such opposition!
Thus making Nature's mercy
seem a merciless thing.

I am a part of the people
who slip into unspoken
confusion and pain
as Spirit is strained from Adam's seed.

What have I to give
but grit-
when I have been plucked and crushed
between the fingers of heaven and earth?

If You Dare

If you dare say
"I want Thee"
then prepare your soul for
chafe and challenge.
He will widen your resolution
or turn it away.

Don't look to the right or left-
nothing will be standing
if you are sincere.

Launch these three words
and they will return
with Heaven's bounty hunter.

This is the Truth,
the unvarnished Truth!
Not for the shy or starry-eyed.

He will make you deep
and grant supernatural substance
to set you apart from
Devil and Death.

Do not speak of why
angels bear arms.
His love is a riddle
and He is a Sphinx
who will ask you the question,
"Do you dare?'

Strike the Drum

It is a dry season.
Come and do a rain dance
over my soul!
Strike the drum of my heart
which wound itself into
one million knots
waiting for your hands.

Everything I am is here
with song and salutation
so come,
for the beat of my heart says-
It is already done.

My East and West await your command,
as my skin has been stretched
over this empty world.
So play, while I've come to my senses
and set them free.

I have given up so many times
but then you strike,
And I realized the music
is not in the drum
but in the drummer.

In this relationship
you are my wealth-
What other joy
could make me abandoned myself
to unknown hands?

My heart spreads like an arid night sky
across the promise of Indra's thunder.

It is the cover you fastened
over the hollow of heaven
and it must resound
while eternity plays
so strike!

Grain of Rice

Oh grain of rice, you are
being cooked by the heat
of this world.

The anger of discontent
will bring you to a boil
until you learn to swallow its fiery ocean
and let the rest pass through you
like steam.

Grow soft with humility, little grain
and rise to the top of this pot
that you may let out
the aroma of the soul.

Then the holy men will come
with their herbs,
and season you
to perfection.

Voices of Vedanta

May their words live in me
and may my being encircle their meaning.
Even as this body is encircled by another,
one of light which is lit by Spirit.

Om. I heard the verse say, "Welcome to God"
for the essence of the Upanishads
is revelation.

You have become my lodestone and I draw near.
You have become my keystone and I find support.
In the endless night of mundane existence,
you shine like the North Star
and show me the way.

Your rivers run
from Him who has authority-
From God to Gods, from Gods to man,
from teacher to pupil, from father to son
from His ocean of grace to the lips of the thirsty
and our thoughts soar in the
Eastern wind.

Even as beauty comes from him who
recognizes beauty, the indweller takes his seat
at the feet of the Vedas.

I have come that Isa may come.
I have come that Kena may come.
I have come that Katha and Prasna may come.
I have come to the master Aitareya,
to the monk Mundaka and to the sage
Svetasvatara who set me ablaze.

Tell me, Taittiriya, what is joy?
Multiply my worth, for I am in love
with the lovers of Brahman.

With cupped hands I have come
to squat beside those Himalayan waters
and drink from centuries of Truth,
poetry and Divine vision.

May the spirit of that sea gather and hold
in these small hands.
For the sacred word is an open boat
for the soul
and a firm grip of wisdom
becomes its oar.

May we be restored like Nachiketas,
like Indra,
like Janaka, King of Videha.
For us may discourse open the door,
inspired, may we walk through.

Om. I heard the verse say, "Thou art That"
and my conscious broke free
to find the feet of the One
who blesses the eye
with Upanisadic vision.

Dissolution and Glory

You are the One who can dissolve all
obstacles as if they were a
sugar cube on your tongue,
But I believe sweetness is ours to taste
when we place our burden
in the solution of your mercy.

It seems there is no such miracle less
in this whole universe, than when you
restore integrity to a
wounded human.

You are the salvation to those
who had the freedom to feel their loss.
We know the glory of all seeking is yours
when Thy drawbridge lowers over those
remote regions of the soul.

You, who part the sea
and the hairs on my head
as one and the same,
remove the shame
from your rebel man.

Oh Fire Divine, Love Divine,
here is your havan! here is your honey!

You have made the wineskin of my heart new
and filled it with the nectar
of your promise-

my words fold in the silence
of your grace.

Rosary of Souls

I am what I've always been,
a channel for Thy imagination.
You are the doer, shaping all things
in this drama of Divine Will.

If I have the freedom to choose,
then I choose to twirl each bead of sandalwood
upon my fingers and say your
precious name.

The way you twirl each bead of my breath
upon your sweet fingers,
And say my name
in your forever rotating
rosary of souls.

Lotus

If I rise up
through the mire, which is dark
from desire and heavy as a heart
which has no thought of God,

If I float free
on the surface like a lotus
where impurity cannot devour
the fragrance of a flower
nor can sorrow settle
on any upright petal,

And in the misted night
with color lily-white,
I shelter the silence and brightness
of the sun,

From blinded fear found
on the bottom;
From the cold and lowly light-forgotten
place, If I could rise,

and open in a crescent-shaped bloom
like the secret, sunlit face of moon
which even ocean could not fathom,

If in another's glory I dare to dream
than I could not lie that I did not rise
but was lifted up

by He who floats my hope
in the compassion of His hand.
My shining soul's command.

I am just a drop of dew
whose water became perfume,
by sitting on the lotus, Kailashananda.

Havan of the Heart

I am beginning to understand.
It has taken so long to begin,
but I am beginning to see the yagna site
and my eyes now want to feast on the flames.

You have made a living temple
in one and all and ordained Intellect
as the priest.
The supreme ritual of sacrifice
must be happening in every atom
and in all matter, it is all that matters.

We need no ghee or rice or mango wood-
for you have made the human heart the best havan
and a content mind its kund.
You have stacked the sticks of man and maya
like a grid stitched upon the air
so your breath can rise from the spaces in-between.

I am beginning to see a presiding deity
standing on the altar of the world
and why giving in to its irresistible call,
my soul smells of camphor and silently waits
to utter "swaha."

Something stirred deep within,
when misfortune became my friction rod.

I am beginning to see the yagna site
through the smoke of contrary eyes.
It is only by the one who dispels darkness,
the splendor of Fire's fire.
By He who rejects the ruby which will not burn
for the havan of the heart.

I take refuge in the match of Kailash.
I take refuge at the feet of puja's flames.

There Is Enough

The speaker is not the one who is full
but the one who is empty.
The writer is not the one with words
but the one with silence and a clean slate.

It is ever the temperament of the world
to fall in a ditch
but the wise do not walk so heavily
upon this earth.

All the iron and brass which armed Goliath
could not save him from
five polished stones and a sling shot.
Bend into the brook and find your stones.

Five doors open to one door,
but one door opens to infinite doors.
Do not waste time looking for a locksmith
when you have the master key!

I know you have been stewing long
in this pot
trying to find
your misplaced love.

But in the still green presence of mind
you are there-
like a creeper continuing its path,
like the slim twin fingers of a fern,
like countless births clinging their leaves
to the tree of life.

What a treasure you are!
I know, for I have seen you in my dreams
and in my noblest visions-
standing like a peacock
fanning your feathers
spanning the four corners of creation.

The conch contains the sound of the ocean,
But You! Your heart contains the song of the soul.
Deities consult its ebb and flow,
and The Good Itself calls that Its throne.

Things are not what they seem,
what a relief-
when nothing here really can fill you fully.
Because the King made you solely
his chalice of bliss.

Look to the hollow road paved in marrow
threading itself through
flowering worlds,
And if you doubt the naked eye of your needle,
ask the Divine Healer-
there is enough.

Touching Down to Fly

Om. May we believe in the believer and His unstoppable love. May we believe in our Self-with courage and strength may we lay down unprofitable deeds. May we believe in alleviation and see our way to compassion. May the tributaries of the four corners pour pure into our breath stream and may that stream feed the larger lake.

He has reached inside His own belief and found us. He invested our souls from where we lay, below the glory of so many crowns. There in the vessel of our heart sits the soma wine. May we uncork it and sip the vineyard which grows out of one grape.

It is I who have merged in the rippling waters of we. It is I who seek the soul of all moveable and immovables. Alone in this vast ocean of Self, may we not fear the immensity which Thou has placed in us!

The multitude wait on a makeshift raft, while The Christ within walks upon the sea. If we think realization is a wing in the wind, may we remember the reason even birds have feet.

Two Birds

I am waiting.
Waiting in the place where you will find me,
someday.
But in the mean while I watch as you move forward-
ever so cautiously and unconvinced.
Like the deer who moves with his eyes on the lion
eager to drink at the watering hole.

I watch as you fumble over your own meaning of me
like a child fumbles in his parents shoes.
And I watch as you race with the gear in reverse
when the stiff wind hits you hard in the back-
but its all forward to me.
When these rises and falls of circumstance move,
its like fingers on a bamboo flute.

Someday you will fly to me, in the place
that you have always known.
But in the mean while it is my delight
as I sit still on this tree
and witness the ant suspend from the fruit-
trying to contrive a way inside.

Plato's Cave

What is the difference between poetry and therapy?
I have been shocked more from dejavu
than any ballpoint pen or acupuncture.

When the lid of time lowers,
and eyes must accustom to a different light,
then I remember that there is something to remember.

So forgive me if I seem dazed
by the kindred spirits of dawn and dusk,
or if I seem a Don Quixote on some obscure
and fanciful mission.
But I believe our worlds balance
on the delicate cusp of a curse and a prayer.

And I ask, who will suffer us to remember
as we walk using words and therapy as crutches
on the edge of a forgotten thing?

For there are some who have not yet
hurt enough to begin to heal.
And some too drunk to believe they drank
the river waters of Lethe.

So what is the difference between
a mission and delusion,
both reside in an inner vision
both have one eye open East.

In my own river mirror I saw
the shelter-slayer of Plato's cave-
filled with blinding eyes of Fire,
frightened by the sight of Sun.

I saw you as the lame
who would scale the mountain,
you as the dumb made eloquent.
I saw others too who would take refuge
in becoming lost or found.

I saw all visions meet at the chin
of a tear-stained face,
where joy and sorrow moved like rivers
feeding in to an ocean of peace.

Therefore I do not know if it is better
to speak so bold,
or to sink into that smooth and able basin
and wait for memory to wash its hands.

The Way of the Bodhisattva

Still I see the spirit of Shantideva
leaving no being alone in their suffering.
He will remain to dispel the misery
of the world.

All my life, Heavenly Fathers did listen
and patient compassion has waited
with a vow to endure the broken pieces of
chest and home.

When will these remains understand
the way of the bodhisattva?

When the reign of Love turns Heart
into a garden of Eden?
When my Self a chariot
for Charity to ride?

But I know neither as I speak imaginations
about those whose hands are fixed
in the mudra of mercy.

And again I ask, who are these missionaries
that live as golden boats amongst men?

They seem to make even the rocks to float
until the last collapsing, sleepwalking sky-
when we may reach across the worlds, palm to palm
and know the continuity of the Soul.

Mere Speculation

I am full of speculation and yet
I have experienced that the paths of
dreams and convenience often diverge.

So it has become a most daring thing,
this curious and precarious human condition.

If I were a prophet I would move men
towards change, away from the rails
of ordinary fate.

But as of yet, The Father has not come, nor has
The Son, nor has the rise of a Holy Spirit-
still, I am full of speculation.

And that urges me on to pick up my
own cross, which is nothing but a
skeleton of tragedy and sin.

In truth, I want no part of this labor
and wait but a voice says,
-Do not faint, as it is your turn-
So I speculate on how many crowns fall
for one facet of His love.

And I look around at a sea of hurt faces,
knowing the burdens of experience and faith.

Either way, it's a daring thing
to gamble with crust and clay,
so let us gleam a bit of Truth.
For, on the grinding lines of a millstone road
what lay? An entire procession
pushing on to a powder.

"Redemption!" some grains say
when crushes come for their dust,
But the axle begins at the hem of His dress.

Song of Moses

When passion and desire set me on fire,
I go to the Guru-he is the cool mountain lake.
When I bathe in his vast expanse,
my vision broadens.

When Moses ascended Mt. Sinai for forty days,
The Children of Israel became restless.
They broke their promise.
They melted down their ornaments and
made a golden idol.

The Omniscient One saw them-self-willed and
of little faith.
His wrath waxed hot
as he sought their destruction.

But Moses, who had found favor with the Lord,
petitioned for the people.
He reminded the Lord of the covenant he made
with Abraham, with Isaac, with Israel.
Moses staved the wrath of the Lord by
his compassion for the people.

Guru is like this.
He leads the lost children
out of bondage, through the wilderness
and to the land of milk and honey-Realization.

Guru teaches the Divine law.
He pacifies the stars on the people's behalf.
He brings gifts of mercy-
without which the impersonal law of God
would see us buried beneath the weight
of our sins.

Who can fathom the good fortune and
undying protection of one who has
the Guru?

His words are like a low lying branch
reaching out over the white waters
of turmoil and disease
before the cascades of Death
sweep us away.

He is the best of beings, the sinless one,
The only one who has found favor
in the eyes of God
and who has become the eye of God.

Struck by his glance, one marvels
For his eyes are the portals to
oceans of space.

He is most assuredly Lord Shiva,
with the cool moon of wisdom
shining on his forehead.

He is endless wealth to the beggar.
Nest and rest for the weary bird.
Even if one be King of all three worlds
but lean on neither Guru nor his staff,
then he is ever the weak and penniless wretch.

Oh Heavenly Father who heard my cry,
where can I find your mercy seat
if not between the gaze of the two
angels poised
on the open petals of my thunderstruck
heart!

Both Weak and Strong

These may be the kind of words
that get burned up
by the breath.

By union or death, tell us Mind, if we be
ring bearers or pall bearers here?

Tell us if you bear the mountain,
like Hanuman, and will serve us
with loyalty until we see Ram.

For it is time to be healed
and the satguru is our soul's sanjivani.
So let us move in a way
that we keep in the company of the givers.

Long we have lived with liars and thieves
and natural are the tears
as we peel back the onion skin
of our inner psychology.

We have had such dreams
in this castle of the Self.
One thousand strange eyes all vied
for the diadem of our will.

But our name is written in His book
pressed like an errant leaf
between the pages of destiny and
choice.

He is our king. And we have come
for His passion, with a spirit
both weak and strong.

We have spoken what was chosen
as our wings cut through
the winds of contrition.

In such tender exchanges there may be
the kind of words
that burn between the lips-

Where the heart's speaking scope
meets with taintless wonder
the silent surrender
of an unfettered breath.

Carry Me Away

Lord, what can my Christ do to find rest?
Die to the thousand deaths of mortal life.

I allowed for one moment the dreaded thought
of death,
and with it the separation from every love.
Of the senses and their objects being ripped asunder,
and I know how much suffering the addict endures.

The meticulous tracking of breath and bone
confounds and confronts man's clinging beliefs.
I thought of my own legion of attachments
and of the undermining rise of spirit from flesh.

I know that consciousness and memory survive things
never again seen by earthly eyes,
And I know there is no sweet rest or repose
in the musty tomb nor on the flaming pyre-
No angel of sleep will numb man's fear.

They say, those who know, that we are
staring down a pit
suspended from a string on which
two mice gnaw.

They say, those who know, that we face
a nest of cobras
while our back is against
a tiger's claw.

They say, those who know, that men
stoned by sensuality
grin with lusty teeth
in the jaws of death.

What can my Christ do to find rest?
Because it is not in what is waking nor in what dreams-
these seem a sheath for the bodily blade.

It is not in the shards of my shattered pain
though I have searched until blood covered my hands.

And it is surely not the wheel of birth and death,
For I have circled the earth a thousand ways.

If He could not pass the cup, though He wished
why would I think or even try?
Sometimes I think His rest is not in man
His rest is born only to die.

In paradise, I ache from root to fruit.
In ocean, I shake from bow to bridge.
Until like a wave of love- My Christ
wakeful and wearily comes
through the forest, with the tide
upon my restless shores to carry me

away.

Hills of Frankincense

The star of Bethlehem is in your heart,
so are the three wise men
below keeping watch.

Above, shines a moon made of ether.
It can show you the path
to Christ, light and wisdom.

But you won't understand this
until your number is up,

Until teacher and student
take their places
and you begin to draw from
an invisible well.

That day will come, my friend
once you've tasted enough devastation.

Once the owl of your intellect
wakes to the night,
you will no longer see Love
as a courtship of fireflies.

Then whatever deeds left
done or undone
won't matter-

An inner vocation will call your works home.

The truth is, you set out with the Sun
long ago
on a journey from East to West,

Somewhere along the way
 you sold the gold,
mingled the myrrh with wine
and forgotten Solomon
on his hill of frankincense.

Lost in the Majesty

Know the secret appetite
of this wheel:

To the eaten, the eater tastes
twice as sweet.

This pen and men are
myrmidons-

They are fuel and fire
and sugar to the stars.

Bondage is a bridge
of ram and fish,

Freedom is the heart
that isn't a mule.

When the water-wheel turns
by extracting power,

Its buckets fill
from a moving stream.

Know this pen and men
are the river,

And their thirst for water
is water's fool.

Know there is hidden
a feast for the soul,

In the season of men
born hungry to know.

For cardamom is the Heart
with spice for its breath
And seeds as black as the
feet of Shyama.

We should want to know
this One, True, Secret source
among us

which swallows and swoons
in the arms of Love.

But time and again, we feel afraid
to save the bel-leaves for
He who takes away.

Lest we spill by his will
into no body-
And remain lost in the majesty
of The Self.

Forever Untouched

Friends, I am caught.

Saturn has cursed me for seven and a half years
and Mars is giving me evil looks.

The tax collector's name?
A black, deathless dragon
with Rahu's head and Ketu's tail.

Now, Karuna is told to be a good puppet,
to enjoy this beautiful world
even the Gods are jealous of.

But she cannot find any joy in that-
as an infidel caught in a stellar web.

the thing is:
He who struggles summons Death.
He who surrenders summons Death too.

My friends, I must confess
The Heart is all I trust-
everything else-a dangerous trick.

For beyond occult science
and the intrigue of stars
is an illuminated Heart,

with twelve vermilion petals
forever touching yet
forever untouched.

Presence and Need

Rarify your desire,
Wisdom, healing and
freedom will flow.

Kailashananda said:
The mind is a bucket-
make it bigger.
The heart is a well-
draw down deep.

I have named Will as the rope
attaching the two,
but detachment determines
what man can hold.

Heaven supplies such a generous ocean
so we must put away our trembling teaspoons
and take our awareness on the
wide open journey of love.

Oh Seeker, I speak of the Atman
of a thirst that is clear and keen,
of Word as the water filling our canteen.

And since we are both drawing
from the same stream, listen
to my heart, but know it is your own.

Passion moves this caravan
of stars and Sundar's camel bells.
The great expanse is man
who wields the powers of presence and need.

My friend, there is a way
to go from tapas to tejase-
but we need a little heat of resistance.

The secret, the wise say,
is all this pain is perfect.

It burns through desire, It burns through effort
It burns through grace into Soul focus.

In other words, the natural law has a back door.
Just relax,
Be receptive in the company of saints,
And affirm with faith- Love is a loadstone
attracting its Self.

Tadvanam

My heart aches
from the tremendous loss
of genuine joy.

All that is sacred and worthy
has left, like a lover in the night
and longing fills the empty chambers
of my soul.

No ocean of sense gives rest
to my wings and on I burn
over waters made salt
by the rain of my tears.

Nothing but Thee can
bring me out of these flames
and release this heart
from rapid decrease.

I fly fast to death's door
but even that volatile, changing gate
cannot erase
the pangs of my separation.

What can the madness of mortality bring
if I am on fire in the fullness of life?

As only the Self can find the Self,
I wait to be led to the river of light.
I wait like one who waits to breathe free.

This cruel delusion has but only
to hear your name,
and cracks from the force
of too kind a word!

Then does the wholeness
no more erode,
and bliss fills the reason
behind any tear.

When anguish heals
by your manifest stay,
I will call you by the name
Tadvanam-
as then will you end
all love-longing.

Surfacing

Guru, one mention of you
and all the lost warriors
of my memory
return.

All these lovesick songbirds return
to nest in the remembrance
of God.

Through and through His Great Desire
moves me-
Always with a spirit of
fight and surrender.

But my heart is like an arrow
you draw back,
the three feathers of faith-
its fletching.

Whereby a thousand winged creatures
lend speed to this dialogue
shot by the outstretched
arm of The Self.

Because you are here, I can't hold back
So come, let me tell you what you already know.

You have released The Spring and The war inside,
The musk deer who runs from pillar to post,
The gathering wave, The compelling change,
The alarm and The dreamer whose
angry to wake.

All these hidden potentials reveal themselves
in your presence-
Each one like a particle of dust
illuminated while moving
before the sun.

You are the only one
who can say where I go from here,
As your pure and masterful feet
stir up the sediment
of these very words
from the vast river of Idea.

Oh my teacher, whatever was said
to the black cloud, say that to me
so I too can watch my weakness leave.
For what good is polite conversation
to one who is in distress!

It is only through your presence
the wide open spaces emerge
which makes even the proud eagle dependant
and waiting, ever waiting
on the wind.

On your uplifting word,
that is why my humanity returns.
While all these other unleashed thoughts
roam the earth
barking at every open hand.

No matter where we stand-
It is Spirit which descends into our perception
Our position remains the same.

So come, Guru, extend yourself through me
with the current of compassion;
that I may be governed and mastered
by the true spontaneity of Love.

For it is not in the calling or coming away-
Kailashananda is The Cause
for this rising up.
Now, there is no explaining
what is happening here.

He is The Salt who melts metal
and evens mind,
until everything else
looses its taste!

How can I relate to this stubborn delusion
that this is no New Age rapture?

I am smoldering inside from everything
I've yet to do.
But Beauty turned many a dancer
to ashes.

From The Three and The Two-
Biswanath, my heart and mind are forever
living at your mercy.

They are like dice you have shaken
and tossed on the table.

Now, I am a king gone beggar.
A weevil in your millhouse,
blinded and buried by
untapped abundance.

But I know what you would say, Master-
In a world full of addicts, who says
healing shouldn't hurt?

So come, Oh Light of Kailash, come closer still
and know-Karuna is lost
in the midst of this love affair.

All that remains are her returning warriors
feeling their way home,

As something in each of us longs
to surface.

Some Divine lightness
up from our inner sea
longs to break-all the rules.

For what we always knew,
long before words,
long before expressions,
long before Truth-with its millions of contradictions-
could segment The Soul.

Guru, one mention of you
and my spirit slips out of reason
and common sense.

Now, All these lovesick songbirds have
unhinged the gates of their
gilded cage,

They have left the eyelashes of The Earth
covered in stardust
and flew, into the arms
of intuitive experience.

The Dialogue

I am the sun the water the wind. Nothing is compromised-when the sun rises the fish don't stop swimming, when the wind blows the bird don't stop singing. Perfect equilibrium am I. All of creation is thriving on my power. I am expansion without form yet I take forms of various states. I am expansion and forever the giver. Unbound freedom is living in me.

*W*hat caused then this great contraction this from the all to the one? What then of this body form? It seems only object an outcast to unity and freedom. It externalizes- it forever watches the sun rise, feels the warmth of the rays and yet it never is the sun. It hears the creatures chirp and sing and yet it is not all creatures but only the one who hears and sees others. It is in exile from bliss and unity and can only receive only receive.

*Y*ou were with me all in all as giver as subject but the desire to see yourself was strong. To experience Nature from the other side- this was the individual asserting its want of experience as object. You were the sun rising, you wanted to see yourself rise! You were the all; you wanted to be the one. The knowledge you ate was of your self and with that came contraction. For now you have only one reference point to view, only one seat you chose to observe what you were-thus contraction and contraction. I grant desires from my love and so you're tasting the desire you plucked from the tree of contraction.

There is great pain and loss from this contraction. I long for the freedom that comes from lack of nothing. I will long for to be the giver and with that not the receiver of this small self for a small means. This viewing is incomplete and the object is disconnected always, it is the wind that tries to catch the dust. The all and all experiences as a partaker of the action and the enjoyment is complete because it is simultaneous with all other acts and would not have to wait for a response. I want this now. I desire expansion and the lasting bliss that only unity can grant.

To be you must only be and not look to observe that being from a selfish eye. The eye is selfish because its only capacity is to receive. The water doesn't rise to see its own waves. Be as the object and you will become that. Forget to see and you will see it all and at the same time. Forget your form and you will be all forms and at the same time. Forget your desires and you will be satiated in the all in all. Then you will expand and expand and the awareness through experience will grow and be far reaching, beyond even your ability to know from such a gross perspective you now possess. The separation between the finite and the infinite is the individual. Lose that one and gain the many.

Glossary

Aitareya - one of the principle Upanishads. Its subject is the process of creation in which all beings, elements, vital airs, senses and intelligence have their source in Spirit as conceived by the one sole Self. lit: at the feet of Master Aitareya

Asana - part of nine-limb system of Raja yoga consisting of specific postures designed to balance body, mind and breath lit: comfortable pose

Atman - the pure Self, supreme consciousness

Bakti - devotion, worship or one who practices the yoga of devotion

Bel leaf - leaf from the Indian Bel tree (aegle marmelos) also called bael, bil, bilva used in religious worship to please Lord Shiva. It has three leaflets, which like Shiva's trident, symbolize the three states of consciousness i.e. subconscious, conscious and Superconscious

Biswanath - name of Lord Shiva meaning one who is "easily pleased"

Bodhisattva - enlightened being who has forsaken final liberation and out of the highest compassion works for the upliftment of all sentient beings

Brahma - God represented as one aspect of the trinity: Brahma the creator, Vishnu the preserver, and Shiva the destroyer

Brahman - the Supreme Cosmic Spirit omnipotent, omniscient, omnipresent

Damaru - a two sided hand held drum with a center knotted string carried by Lord Shiva; when rotated it represents the dualistic aspect of nature resonating the single divine sound, AUM

Devi - goddess

Don Quixote - day-dreaming knight in the Cervantes novel by same name

Four-fold goal – radiant health, long life, prosperity material and Divine Bliss

Goliath - biblical warrior giant who fought against David. David defeated him with a sling-shot and a stone which struck Goliath right between the eyes

Govinda – name for Krishna lit: protector of the cows

Guru - spiritual preceptor lit: remover of darkness

Hanuman - monkey god of the Ramayana who helped Sri Rama battle the evil Ravana He is the symbol of benevolent service from a disciplined mind

Havan - special mixture of herbs offered in Hindu fire worship services

Hrishikesh - name for Krishna in the Bhagavad Gita meaning "he who has his senses controlled"

Isa - one of the principle Upanishads, lit, "Lord of the Universe." This brief but potent Upanishad proclaims the glories of Spirit and differentiates between knowledge and action and the immanent and the transcendent.

Indra - great defender of both gods and mankind. Indra is considered the strongest of beings, the greatest of warriors and the God of lightening and storm

Janaka - wise king and sage from the famous debates in the forest (Brihadaranyaka Upanishad). His keen unswerving questions were presented to Saint Yagnavalka in order to gain knowledge of hidden Truths

Japa - repetition of mantra either silently or out loud. Usually performed on a rosary indicated for prayer

Jiva - individual soul of man

Kailash - mountain in the Himalayas thought of as the abode of Lord Shiva

Karma - universal law of cause and effect which is said to be the driving force of destiny

Karuna - compassion

Katha - one of the principal Upanishads in which the young, but wise Nachiketas received discourse and teachings from the Lord of Death-Yama

Kena - one of the principal Upanishads in which the Spirit Supreme wins a victory for the gods

Ketu - south node of the moon astrologically called Dragon Tail, known for its malefic impact. According to Vedic mythology, Rahu/Ketu were once a demonic dragon who tried to disguise herself as a god in order to become immortal. When Lord Vishnu discovered her deception he sliced her in half, hence Dragon Head and Dragon Tail. see Rahu

Krishna - eighth incarnation of the Lord Vishnu lit: the dusky one (due to his dark complexion). Teacher and charioteer for Arjuna in the Bhagavad Gita

Kund - metal bowl used for placing wood during the Hindu ritual of fire worship

Lila - divine sport in which creation is seen as The Lord's play

Lethe - according to Greek mythology, one of the five rivers in the underworld. Souls who drink its waters forget everything hence it is the river of forgetfulness

Mantra - sacred phrase repeated for its physical, psychological, mental and spiritual healing properties. Mantra repetition is a clear science that forms specific vibratory patterns from the substratum of all matter i.e. sound, the first sound being-OM

Maya - sanskrit term meaning illusion; the veiling power of nature covering universal reality of God

Moses - biblical servant of The Lord who led the children of Israel out of Egypt and initiated them into the Divine Constitution

Mouna - vow of silence

Mount Sinai - mountain in which Moses divinely received the Ten Commandments from The Lord

Mudra - a symbolic seal often done by the hands of a Yogi to represent higher ideas of benevolence, The God Head and the seat of The Self. The main mudra known as Chin Mudra forms a lock for the flow of energy in the body during meditation. It is seen as the index finger bent down to meet the thumb forming the circle of positive and negative energy. This represents the circle of unity with all, or yoga

Mundaka - a principal Upanishad lit: at the feet of the Monk. Sage Angiras speaks on the lower wisdom of Vedic ritual and of those who pass beyond into the higher wisdom which cannot be attained through action

Nachiketas - from the Katha Upanishad. The noble son of Vajasravasa who boldly held discourse with the Lord of Death

Nataraja - one of Lord Shiva's forms in which he embodies the cosmic dancer. Hatha yoga is thought to have its origin from Nataraja as he forms the eight million four hundred thousand species of life in his dance of creation

Omkarum- Om. The primeval sound of God from which all creation is said to have sprung from

Praseed – lit: be pleased. The word used in prayer addressing the Divine Mother

Prometheus - Greek god who gave the gift of fire to mankind. He tricked the gods into eating bare bones instead of good meat and stole the sacred fire from Zeus and the gods

Puja - Hindu ceremonial worship with flowers, fruits, prayers and other offerings given symbolically to the Lord

Purusha - pure consciousness of man. The Soul or The Self of all beings

Rahu - north node of the moon astrologically called Dragon Head, known for its malefic impact. According to Vedic mythology, Rahu/Ketu were once a demonic dragon who tried to disguise herself as a god in order to become immortal. When Lord Vishnu discovered her deception he sliced her in half, hence Dragon Head and Dragon Tail. see Ketu

Ram - seventh incarnation of Vishnu and hero in the Indian epic poem, The Ramayana, in which Sri Rama slays the demon king Ravana

Rishikesh - lit: valley of saints. Located at the foothills of the Himalayas in Northern India

Rudra - Lord Shiva in the aspect of the destroyer

Sanjivani - life restoring herb used in The Ramayana to bring Laxman, the brother of Rama, back to life

Sapera - name given to the snake charmers of India

Satguru - lit; the true guru

Shakti - feminine power of creation

Shantideva - eighth century Indian Buddhist saint and author of The Way of the Bodhisattva

Shiva - God represented as one aspect of the trinity: Brahma the creator, Vishnu the preserver, and Shiva the destroyer

Shyama – lit: the dark one. Another name of Lord Krishna

Sita - consort of Sri Rama who was kidnapped by the demon king Ravana in the epic poem, The Ramayana

Solomon - biblical king, son of David, known for his wisdom, wealth and writings

Soma - mentioned in Vedic literature as both intoxicating ambrosia and a god personified. The metaphor here being that of consciousness ever filled with the immortal wine of Divine Bliss

Sundar - name of Lord meaning "the beautiful one"

Surya - the Sun god who enlightens both heart and mind by destroying the darkness of sins and bad karma

Svetasvatara - one of the principal Upanishads glorifying Brahman as the Supreme Reality

Swaha - word uttered upon making an offering especially in fire worship lit: I offer my heart unto you

Tadvanam - name of The Lord lit: the end of all love longing

Taittiriya - one of the principal Upanishads concerning the nature of joy

Tapas - austerity and purification performed as sacrifice with the aim of burning sins and one's lower nature

Tejase - effulgence or radiant light emanating from the Yogi who has reached a high level of purity

Upanishads - end of the Vedas. Spiritual revelations on the Spirit of the Universe, or Brahman, composed by various saints and sages with the earliest documents being between 800 and 400 B.C.

Vedanta - school of Indian philosophy based on Vedic teachings which emphasizes Intellect as a means to develop discrimination and dispassion which culminates into realization of a non dualistic Truth

Vedas - lit: book of knowledge. They are the oldest scriptures known to man, divided into four books: the Rig Veda, the Yajur Veda, the Sama Veda and the Atharva Veda

Vishnu - God represented as one aspect of the trinity: Brahma the creator, Vishnu the preserver, and Shiva the destroyer

Yagna - Hindu religious ceremony in which prayers and oblations are offered into a sacred fire. Yagna performance holds great symbolic significance in terms of inner sacrifice as one's ego is offered to the God within

Yama – referred to here as the god of death

Yoga - lit; union or to yoke. Yoga is a systematic means, path and end result of unifying one's Self with the Divine